Thoughts of a Rose

Kianti` Ayshea`

Cover Art By: Stormy

This One's for You

I would like to take the time out I feel to say THANK YOU to everyone who has contributed to my spiritual evolution, regardless of your contribution. Words would never be able to express the amount of gratitude in my heart. To my soul tribe thank you for always being there when I need someone to talk to. We always have the greatest time. To the young girls and women out there in the mist of a struggle PLEASE keep your head up. Things with time will get better. My son, TJ, you are mommy's biggest motivation. It is because of you that I have found the strength within myself to never in a million years give up. I want you to know that you can do anything you set your heart to.

Thunder Storm or Sun Shower?

Lately I've been feeling like my time is ticking. It's almost as if I live with the consistent thoughts of "Where is my life going?" "What is my purpose?" "When will my journey begin?" "When is enough, enough, or too much, too much?" Everyday these are things I wonder about. For so long I took so many things, people and opportunities either for granted or too lightly! "All apart of growing up"...I thought, "What's meant to be will always find a way." That could've helped if something, anything found a way. Is it that my journey has yet to start or is it that this is how my life is supposed to be? Full of screw ups and questions as to why. The answer to that is all of these screw ups, questions and lessons learned on a daily basis is what my journey consists of. Every day that I live, I am experiencing my journey. Every time that I mess up, I am learning new lessons to apply to my daily encounters. I understand that now, and I embrace every second of my traveling experience with open arms, an open heart, and an open mind. There is no limit as to how far I can go. All I have to do is believe, have faith and never give up.

Growing up, my mom was someone I definitely looked up to. She was young, beautiful, so full of life and vibrant energy, but most importantly, she was strong! She did whatever was in her power to get the things that were necessary done. I admire her for these qualities. I call her "Wonder Woman". For the first four years of my life, it was just us three. My grandma Ada and Granddad Walt both played huge roles in my life as well. My dad was someone who I also admired to a certain extent. He met my mom when she was roughly five months pregnant with me, fell madly in love with her, and has been apart of my life ever since. Don't quote me on those details, I just know that it was for the most part along those lines. It takes a strong man to step up to the plate that someone else left at the table, my dad and I were joined at the hip. I remember when I was that age, I loved Mary J. Blidge, dad would record home videos of me singing to her songs, as young as I was I knew all of the lyrics as if they were my own. My sister was born in March of 1995. I remember my grandmother and I went to the hospital because my mom had just given birth, and I was so excited. When we got back to the house, it was in flames. I watched my grandmother talk to the firemen and police officers that were on the scene. I have very few memories of what happened in that house, because shortly after that incident we moved elsewhere. I was excited to be a big sister. Shortly after she was born, the relationship between my parents got rough. Being young I tried to somehow in my mind cover up the reality of what was going on. My mom and dad were in love, but I learned at a very early age that love sometimes just isn't enough as I watched them fall out of it. You have to prove it. You have to mean it. You have to be there! My dad was heavily involved in some things that my mom just couldn't approve of. She cared about him and often worried about the direction in which his life was headed, she by all means had no interest in having a part in it. Their relationship dwindled away, my sister and I were now children of a broken home. It honestly to me at the time meant nothing, or so I thought. I lived my life according to everyone else's schedule. There were days to be at dads, and days to be at moms. There was even a period where we went to school in the city that he stayed in for a while, and then transferred to another school where she was. Eventually the things my dad were doing caught up with him and we were living with mom permanently. While my sister and I thought our dad had been gone for so long because he was "driving a truck", he was really incarcerated for doing things he apparently shouldn't have. Once I found out the truth about what was really happening, I came to grips with the fact that I knew all along. I recall seeing him do things before that were suspicious. I thought back to the time I walked in on him and his friends in the room with some stuff I thought was powder. I was mentally beyond my years. I knew something was off about that, I was right. We would go to my grandparent's house on the weekends, and while we were there, we would all go visit my dad. I would use that hour to try to share with him as much as I possibly could in regards to school and what I thought at that age was my social life. I couldn't wait for him to come home he always knew what to say to cheer me up. It seemed as if it was taking an eternity.

One day my sister and I were outside riding our bikes, and I notice this man sitting in a car across the street watching us. My mother would never let us go too far, and was standing right on the opposite corner. I could see her from where we were, and started rushing back to tell her what I saw. I told her about the man sitting in his car just watching us. She started to tell me she knew who he was. He got out of his car, I was scared. I had no idea who he was and you can only imagine how protective I was of my mother and sister. It was just us. I got closer to her and made sure I could see my sister in my view. He started talking to me asking me how I was, and telling me how pretty I was. If it wasn't for my mom standing right there and me having the trust for her that I did, I would have been completely freaked out. He then asked my mother if he could walk me to the store, she agreed to it saying "You better not go any further than the store, and I am going to stand here and watch you as you go." The entire time we were walking he kept asking me questions about school, and the things that I liked, meanwhile I'm in my head trying to figure out what gives him any right to ask me any of this. We get back to my mother and I try to make it as obvious as I can that I was uncomfortable, but it didn't seem like anyone was catching on. It started getting dark out, so we went in the house. My grandmother invited this man in too.

As we are all in the living room, I am sitting down about to eat my sandwich as they talk amongst each other. I then hear my grandmother say to my mom "Just ask her, she is a smart girl. I'm sure she will know." My mother then turns to me with the look of worry and concern in her eyes, and asks me "Do you know who this is?" pointing to this man. I looked back at her, then looked at everyone in the room, and said "My father." She replied hesitantly "Yes." From then on out things were weird for me. I just found out that my dad was in jail, and now an even bigger bomb that someone else is my parent. I found out I had another sister and a brother from him as well. He would come around ever so often to take me to see them, or to try to introduce me to his world. I must have made it really tough on him, because after a while I didn't see him anymore. It wasn't until years and siblings later that I heard anything of or from him again. He and I to this day do not have a relationship, and the only father I know is the one who was there since day one. That is the man I respect.

In 2001, I lost my grandmother. We were really close, and it was something I honestly thought I would never heal from. Even though I had my own room, I slept in my grandmother's room every night. She smoked cigarettes, and the smell would clog my nostrils as I was trying to sleep, but ironically it was my favorite place to be. My mom worked a lot of hours, and she was in school too. She made time for me and my sister whenever she could, but I was with my grandmother while my mom was reorganizing her life, and being the amazing example that she was. One day while sleeping in my grandmothers room as usual, I was waken up by loud screams of pain. My grandmother was hunched over the side of the bed saying how badly it hurt. My aunt was standing there crying and holding my grandmother up while on the phone with 911. As I panicked in fear of what was going to happen next, my intuition told me something wasn't right. As the ambulance made its way, my grandmother asked me to sweep the house. I gladly did what she asked me to. They arrived, and took my grandmother out of the door and into the emergency vehicle. I went back into the house with my sister and my uncle. We spent all of 30 minutes in his room and my dad's parents came to pick us up and bring us to their house for the night at my mother's request. I had a really hard time sleeping that night. I just wanted to know what was wrong with my grandmother. The next morning I woke up to my grandmother calling me and my sister downstairs to the kitchen for breakfast. As we were watching our favorite cartoons the phone rang, and it was my mother saying she was on her way. I insisted on talking to her, which to this day I am thankful that I did. I heard it all in her voice what was about to happen next, but I prayed for the best. When my mom got there, she turned the television off and said she wanted to talk to us. She took extremely long breaths, and her face was pale. She then began to look dizzy I suggested she take a seat. She proceeded to tell us that my grandmother passed away. I put my head down and cried to myself, which gradually turned to me sobbing aloud. That was the first time I had ever really felt my chest tighten from pain. It was in that moment I knew exactly what the pain of losing someone you loved felt like. I had months of sleepless nights due to crying my heart out. My grandmother was my roll dog so to speak. Where ever she was, I was. With losing her I experienced my first heart break.

Shortly after my grandmothers passing my mother started dating her best friend, who to this day is my step father. He was a cool guy in my opinion. He had a good job, he was in college getting a degree, he took care of all of his loved ones, and most of all he made my mother happy. I had never seen her as happy as she was once they started seeing each other exclusively. He was very respectful of the fact that she had two children, and was willing to contribute in any way that he could, even though my mother made it very clear it was not a necessity for him to do so. My opinion on him, the way you are reading it now was not always like this. This is my maturity speaking. Me being an adult now with a sound mind and knowing what matters, I get it. Being as though my dad was in prison, I found out he wasn't my birth father and my grandmother passed away all within a year I wanted to keep my mother as close to me as I could. I was in a very dark state in my life, and whenever I would try to express that to someone, their rebuttal would be along the lines of I'm a child and I need to get over it. As if because I was a kid that I didn't know how I felt. Eventually my mom got tired of fronting all of the bills in the house where she was responsible for the mortgage all the way down to the groceries. Apparently these duties went beyond a parent's automatic responsibility of their children, she was taking care of her adult siblings as well. My now step father stepped in, and we moved in with him. My step dad and I got along for the most part. I honestly think being a man and coming into a picture where there are two children, maybe he felt he had something to prove, but we bumped heads a lot. A lot of the time it would be because my sister and I would be joking around with him, and he would take it extremely far. I knew that he loved my mom, and I knew she loved him too, but in my head no one could replace my father. So when he would try to discipline me, it wouldn't work, and I could only imagine how frustrated that must have made him. One day my mother called me and my sister into the kitchen, so we came and sat down. Keep in mind everything that I was already going through in such a short amount of time, and how I was feeling before I tell you what came out of her mouth next. She then told us that she noticed how we would treat her significant other, and that she felt we were being extremely disrespectful. I attempted to let her know that we didn't mean anything by it, and that sometimes we felt he would take things out of context. I was in a really bad space and just wanted to make sure that we were okay. She interrupted me to tell me that she was finally happy, and that if she had to choose between us and her happiness, she would choose her happiness. For a child that is already very emotionally, mentally and spiritually ill due to a series of recent events, I don't think that was helpful to my healing in any way. It actually harmed me more. It caused me to lash out. I was completely numb and the next 6 years of my life proved that in every way.

My mom is a sweet woman she has a heart of gold. I know that she was happy and wanted to keep It that way, but I to this day do not agree with what she said, or how she went about it. To each his or her own I suppose. However, whenever I need her guidance, she is always there right on time. She always gave us the "real" on things. Some people may think or feel we knew certain things too early, but I feel we needed the knowledge. I appreciate it all the time. Without knowing half of the things that I knew, I could have been a potential victim to some things. People around me were gang banging, selling drugs, and some were even selling their bodies. Allow all of this to sink in, because let's keep in mind we were children. Having all of these things around me had me feeling like I had to be more than what my environment intended for me to be. Along the way, I stumbled and made several mistakes. The first of many thinking I knew more than I did too soon, and allowing the things that hurt me to create a monster within myself. I was so blinded by my pain that I did many foolish things. I let it take full control of me and the situations I got myself into. Of course I didn't go out there looking for it, but in a way I invited it. The things I did and said the thoughts that I had caused a lot of what happened to me. I believe my mother had good intentions just as any good parent does. I was just an independent being on an intense search for my soul.

I have always known that I was blessed with many talents, following my heart being my favorite one! When I want something, I mean really desire something- I chase it down. I will claim what is mine, and do whatever it takes to make it all worth it. The problem with that though is, knowing the talents you have, and knowing what your heart is like. I couldn't quite figure out which talent to sharpen first. In other words, I couldn't figure out how I should use each one. Hand in hand with that "problem" is the fact that I love to help and be there for others. However, sometimes I get so wrapped up in helping and being there for others that I often forget myself. The things that matter to me somehow get placed on the back burner. Well, I refuse to live that way any longer. I will be myself, I will love people and continue to be there, but I am making a promise to be there for myself first. Knowing the direction that I want my life to go in, I will follow thru with what I start! I will combine all of my talents and write a book dedicated to all people searching to find themselves. Wondering when or how they will get out. People who are tired of living in question, that are willing to take life by the horns and enjoy the ride. This is me welcoming you into my world. The most intimate things about my self are soon to be exposed. How do I feel? I feel like God put me through it so that I could pull other people through. I understand thoroughly that everything works together for the greater good.

I may not be where I'm supposed to be just yet but God promised, and I believe because he promised! Your enemies shall become his enemies. Remain obedient. When you think you don't know, he already does. His angels heard the enemy and made the plan. You shall not bow down!

Sometimes, all a person needs is comfort. I find mine in mental stimulation due to intellectual conversation, laughing, dancing, reading a book, or writing. Instant comfort to the soul, writing is my usual go to. It's my outlet and overall way of getting things off my chest that I cannot otherwise mainly because I have always felt misunderstood. Inconveniently, I've also put others and their happiness above my own, ultimately leaving me to be sad and feel alone. Now that I think about it, all of this came from that one terrible thing said to me as a child. I felt like my happiness came last if it even came at all. Until one day I realized that if I am not at my best, I can't possibly assist others, the things that I've experienced and grown through cross my mind constantly. The only difference is I no longer allow things and events from my past to cause strain on my present or future. I'm still working through it, currently on a spiritual journey, learning the significance and art of alignment and balance. I still make mistakes daily, as I still do not have all of the answers. The ones I do though, I plan to share with the world. Someone needs me, and I did mention how I feel about that. For as long as I could remember, people have always been at ease with coming to me about anything. That has helped me to continue being the kind and warm hearted individual that I am. It actually taught me how to embrace those qualities about myself. If people allowed the things they endured to change them, it's because they were consumed by their problems. My present goal is to apply my wisdom earned to any new experiences I may face.

Enjoy the little things, try your best not to over think. Minimize the situations, people and things that don't contribute to your growth. Maximize the things that do. Way too often I found myself caught up in a whirl wind of irrelevant factors. Eventually learning how to jump out of the hell fire, it was torture. There was no way possible I would progress, while my mind was stuck in those places and on those events. It's okay to not have all of the answers, but it is not okay to become complacent and not seek them. I have stood firmly in my belief that I am more than what others may classify me as. Ultimate Zen is my goal, there will be obstacles. My focus is on the ways I will overcome them, and not stress that they exist. In fact, I am learning to appreciate them. Out of everything experienced, there is a lesson of value to be learned. In life when we don't quite learn the lesson the first time, we will find ourselves faced with a similar if not the same issue later on down the line. Consider those tests to be gems of wisdom, fitting perfectly into your crown. I wear mine with pride, and you should too!

I've seen it way too many times where a person allows life and loss to change their spirits. I know from experience how difficult it can be to stay positive through all of life's trials and tribulations. Surprisingly though, those around me are never able to tell when I'm having a really rough time. So many people see me as this radiant and confident woman, who's always in the best possible mood, and that is not always the case. Despite what everyone may think, I have had several lower than low points in my life. Since about age 10, I have quietly battled a sever case of depression. I have even had the thought of leaving this world behind more than a few times. Whenever I got close to actually taking my own life, there was a great deal of hesitation. I have always felt like there was a greater purpose for my life. And that it wasn't fair to whatever that was, for me to be selfish. It was almost as if someone that I didn't even know was depending on me to survive. Being a parent has given me more than enough reason to survive, but I also do it for all of those women who no longer desire to be here. Nobody knows what you're dealing with because you suffer in silence. I want it to be known that I am here for you. Trust that I will never be the person to turn my back on another person in need, especially not a woman. We have it really hard out here, and people sleep on that way too often. If for whatever reason anyone needs me, I make myself more than available. It is what I was called here to do. I was called to spread self enlightenment, encouragement, wisdom, peace, joy and love through my written and spoken word.

Sometimes in life, you have moments where you feel completely alone. You have gone through so much, and continue to face obstacle after obstacle on a daily basis. No one shares the same story, as all of ours is different. Do not ever allow anyone to tell you or make you in anyway feel like you don't matter, you do. We were all sent here for a reason, whether or not we have gotten to that point in our lives where we comfortably know what that is or not. All you have to do is remain strong, one day everything will all make sense. I know from speaking with other people that my story is far from the worst, but that doesn't make my story any less relevant. The things that I went through at such a young age are things that cause suicidal deaths every day. People feeling like that have literally no outlet. Everything being kept inside can drive a person mad. Have you ever heard a story about a young child who robbed someone, killed someone, beat someone up, sold drugs, fast in the ass etc. and the first thing everyone says is "That child is lost."? It's so true. They are lost, and there is a great chance that at one point or another they attempted to speak to someone, anyone, and no one listened. One thing I never want to do to my son is something I feel adults and parents do way too often. I never ever want my son to feel like because he is a child that his thoughts, opinions, or feelings are invalid. He matters and he will until the day I stop breathing and beyond know that he is important. When he thinks something, I want to know his thoughts. When he wants to get something off of his chest, I want to listen to his feelings. If he has a dream, I will assist him by giving him the necessary tools to make it happen, to achieve his greatness. He is worthy of all that his heart desires. We all are. Who ever said that we have to become less than because of the things we go through? No one and who ever did is a damn lie.

By me writing this to you, I am planting the seeds. As you continue to flip through the pages, you are watering those seeds. Allow my confidence to jump out of these pages into your spirit. I will be your daily motivation if nothing else. As you hold this book in your hands, understand and realize this is something I did for myself. I rose above everything that people have done to me, and strive to be and have more. I do this for so much more than myself; I do this for all of you. When the universe says do it, you do it! If you find yourself reading this, understand that this is no accident. I was meant to share myself with you, and you were meant to read it. You will get something out of this. If nothing else I want you all to know anything is possible! STAY FOCUSED! If you remain strong, everything will work together for your benefit! YOU ARE MORE THAN YOUR CIRCUMSTANCES SAY YOU ARE!

Pushing Forward For Success!

At one point in time, it felt as if everything was falling apart. My mom and I weren't Seeing eye to eye, she wanted me to do things her way and I wanted to find my own. When I moved away from home for the first time, I did so with $8.00 in my pocket and moved to Chapel Hill, North Carolina. All I knew was that I felt extremely restricted my entire life up to then, and I was willing to be without materialistic things in order to discover myself and who I was. For many years thereafter, I remained lost with minimal sense of direction. I was done living every second of my life according to someone else's "rules". However, it seemed for a while that the only way I would survive was if I followed suit. Meaning, I would have to follow regulations regardless of if they came from my mom, a boss at a job, or the government. Naïve, I fell into the trap. Ever since I was a little girl, I knew that there had to be more to life. I wanted to grow up and sing, dance, write, have my own business. I wanted to do everything but work for someone else. I learned very early in life, that often times it's not about what's fair. It doesn't matter if it's right or not, there has been a system placed in "order" that restricts people from being their true selves. The only difference between the garbage man and a superstar is one of them had the courage to go after their dreams while the other fell victim to the systems say so. When we are children, we have vast imaginations that are shut down very early by people, parents included, telling us that certain things are not real or not true. What makes those things true? Who said they aren't real, and who made them "in charge" of anything? I was determined to make a way out of no way. To this day that is a mentality that I keep, because I know that you attract things to yourself. You attract these things with the thoughts that you have and the emotions that you feel. I remember having a job one day, and losing it the next. Over bull, I would lose my jobs. Then again too, for a really long while I would think about things after they had been said and done. Now as I have grown, I find myself faced with a lot of similar situations, but I handle them differently. Always remember that no matter how hard times may be for you, they won't stay that way forever. $8.00 to my name, in a completely different state, not eating for days at a time, I made a way, simply by remaining positive. When I dealt with the father of my child, I had to bust my chops to make sure my child and I had a roof over our heads. No matter how hard I tried to maintain and keep everything afloat, I became a single mother. Shortly after, I lost my job, and simply put, could no longer afford such an expensive place. The plan was never for me to have done it alone, yet I was way before the separation even came to pass. I had to downsize my living space, and manage my expenses closely. I remained positive. I was unemployed for about a week before I found another job. I moved in the apartment upstairs from my grandmother, which is cool, because rent is nowhere near as expensive as it once was. I had a really decent job that was helping me keep everything together. I believed that I hit the jack pot, being as though it was a corporate office, and I was able to successfully handle all responsibilities. About six months of me being there, and three months after I began walking in my purpose, I started to feel as if I didn't want to be there anymore. The job was literally draining my energy and I thoroughly understand that my energy has to be conserved so that it can be utilized for my purpose. The job was moved out of my path. See, jus as everything aligns, it serves a purpose. Things happen exactly as they should, when they are supposed to happen. One morning I woke up and felt completely at ease, which would sound strange to someone else, because it was thirty two minutes past my start time at work. I am beyond convinced that if my mom would not have called me when she did, that I would have waken up much later than that. While she was in panic mode, I was completely calm. I got up and began to get myself and my son together for the day. I dropped him off at school, and went to work. I went through the day doing my normal and consistent tasks. While on the phone with one of the customers, I kept having my attention shifted to this tree that was outside across the street. Being as though this had been my desk for months, I wanted to look up the symbolism of this tree, as I had to know why I was drawn to it. "The wisdom of balance, promise and practical magic." Is what it said. For a while, I was feeling as though I couldn't put as much of my energy into my writing, because it was being drained by the people and things that took place at that job. At about 2 o' clock that day, my manager called me into the office, and we had our final discussion. This time around it was unlike any other, immediately, I felt a release of pressure, simply because, it was overall weighing down on me. I wasn't at all sure of how I was going to make ends meet, but I had this firm understanding that everything was going to be okay. The week after I got released, I went away for a weekend, one of the best vacations of my life. I kept that feeling for about 2 weeks, and during that time, I proceeded doing what Earth Angels do. Being the ear and shoulder that everyone needs, my energy was yet again being drained, but in this time, a completely different way. The importance of recharging ones energy is serious and for about 8 days there was no reciprocation. Don't get me wrong, I have an amazing group of spiritually enlightened individuals around me, but at this time I felt it was more important for me to give energy to them, rather than to receive it. That is until I had a break down, which was completely unexpected and clearly my body's way of letting me know that I need time to recuperate. So I decided to re-center, and refocus my energy where it needs to be. I have to remember that all I am enduring is because I need to be the example others need. I go through pain alone so that others don't have to. The main goal here is to be the extended hand that so many aren't fortunate enough to have. I know what it feels like to be alone, and I don't want anyone to feel like that if they don't have to. Understand that I am bringing you on my journey with me for that reason there is hope, you just have to understand that. In the mist of this journey, I had a moment of complete and utter vulnerability. I felt as if my dreams and goals may have to be put on hold to maintain my responsibilities. I was sending out over 20 copies of my resume a day, and had only 1 interview in 3 weeks. One of which, was made to seem as if I had the job, only to find out a couple of days later that they decided to go with another candidate. All of this was hurting me, because I'm the type of person who grinds and gets results. I forgot what it feels like to be in a space like this. All I need is a part time job that pertains to my purpose, and allows me the time necessary to focus on my writing, my love. I allowed material and fabricated needs to consume my mind. It doesn't even stop there. The father of my child was being his self and insinuating that I don't bring our child back to where he currently resides. Then one day, I went to the park to do some writing, meditating, nature walking, and I cleared my mind and allowed my pineal gland to stretch. I get to my son's school just to find out that he's having difficulty breathing, so I rushed him to the doctor's office. While there, the doctor let me know that my son has asthma, I was on the brink of losing my mind. Not only were my finances not where I would have liked them to be, but I couldn't do what I really wanted to, which was write because bills were saying I needed more income, then my son was diagnosed with asthma. When I went to fill his father in on what was going on, I sent photos and videos, text messages and I even called. His father however, as usual, was worried about everything but the topic at hand which is our son. I had to endure that alone. Which, I have come to accept that even though I did not make this child alone, I am raising him alone, I break my back alone. Where we are right now, is my son having to take oral meds twice a day for five days, and get on his nebulizer every four hours. His breathing needs to constantly be checked and we are headed back to the doctor for a follow up visit soon. I am utterly exhausted, yet couldn't rest even if I really wanted to. After leaving the doctors office, I can honestly say that I felt extremely light. My son is not 100% better, but he is indeed feeling, behaving, and breathing better. As a mother, I know that we always want the absolute best for our children, so when they are not at their best, it's heart aching. However, I understand the importance of remaining strong for them. Our children have the ability to feed off of our energy, therefore I choose to give off nothing but the highest and most positive vibrations. I will instill in my son those very characteristics. I want my son to grow up knowing that what you give out is what you get back. My mind state is nine out of ten times that of positivity, regardless of what I may be faced with at the time. Not too long after getting back from the doctors office, I received a phone call asking me to come in for a job interview, and I accepted. Being in this particular hardship that I am in, does not prevent me from looking forward to all of the many great things that I know the universe and God have in store for me. Whenever things appear to be going "bad" reevaluate your thoughts and emotions. The reason I say that, is because your thoughts, feelings, even your actions have a bigger role in the situations you deal with than many realize. Always remember, I speak from experience only. When I focused on the bad things, people, situations etc., more of those things came to pass. Yet, when I paid more attention to the good in my life, even something as simple as being able to pick a pen up and write, many more good things crossed my path. The interview went really well, the overall vibe in that place was really good. It's important to read and observe the energy around you. In addition, one must be extremely careful with the things and people they exchange energy with. The people in there were extremely down to earth, and I could honestly see that being an amazing and suitable work space for me. The work that would be required of me is nothing unmanageable or energy draining. Prior to leaving, the manager let it be known that her and her partner really liked me a lot, and the only other approval we needed was that of the business owner himself. Granted, the energy in the building was great, but this is still a job market, so it is now a waiting game. Partly the reason I am making sure I have residual income to support my family and future endeavors. A few days have gone by, and I started to manifest things I wanted for myself. Anytime a negative thought would attempt to enter my mind, I began thinking three positive thoughts. Although I went in there and smashed the interview, I was told I would be called by the end of that day and I wasn't. Normally, one would begin to wonder if the interview went as well as they thought, but I knew better. I knew there was a reason for me not receiving the call back on that day. After an evening of laughter and conversation with my best friend, I concluded that I would be receiving the call that I was waiting on and that the job I desired and at this time would require would be mine. I woke up feeling extremely "blah", however decided to do a follow up call with the place of interest. She confirmed that she had yet to speak with the person making the decision, and that she would let me know when that was later on in the day. I made breakfast for my son and I, who by the way still doesn't have much of an appetite. I cleaned the kitchen, and then I came to my room and went to sleep. At 2:32pm I received a phone call letting me know that the position I applied for had been given to someone else. However, they wanted to bring me on the team as an editor. To my understanding, the position I applied for was the only one available, in lament terms, the universe will make sure that everything aligns as it should, and always on time. I gladly accepted the offer. Such a weight has been lifted as I now know that my mind is such a powerful tool, and with that, my heart and the universe backing me up, I'll never lose. When you are walking in your purpose, the universe will let you know it. One day at random, I received two sweet sonnets from two women who are inspired by and admire my work. I was still blown away by the universal law of attraction. When I say the universe will let you know, that is exactly what I mean. So you mean to tell me that I have always dreamed of making writing my career, and now not only am I self publishing my first of many books, and the magazine I write for going print, but my 9 to 5 also aligns with my purpose. I am overall humble and so thankful to be able to bring all of you along for the ride. My intentions are to let people know they can do anything with persistence, dedication and faith. What better way to do that than to lead by example? When dealing with difficult times, one must remember the good and faithful quote "Tough times don't last, tough people do." I will never pretend to haven't ever doubted myself, because I have. I have been confused, I have felt pressured. I have experienced some of the worst anxiety attacks, I know what it means to not always have been positive. However, I can honestly say that once I changed my outlook on life, everything not only looked different, but became different as well. One may be reading this and thinking to themselves "she sure is repeating things", but that's because I know repetition is the key to learning and knowledge is the key to success. Everyone can change their mind set, if they allow themselves to do so. You may have been stuck in a certain chapter in your life, not knowing how to pull yourself out or how to start anew. All of that is due to what you see around you. Let's face it, a lot of us don't know what it means to only feel, see, and believe the best because we have become accustomed to being the under dogs. Anything that you want, you can have. We tend to put an overload of pressure on ourselves to be the next "Michael Jordan" or "Oprah", instead of simply being the best possible version of ourselves. It won't by any means be easy, especially knowing how much we will have to change or reconsider to get ourselves to where we want to be. It requires discipline and determination. You will not be able to do the things you've always done, you will not be able to keep the same family and friends around you. The difficulty with that is nobody wants to be alone. We are human and enjoy companionship. Truth is though, that not everything and everyone is meant to be apart of the next chapter or chapters yet to come. Get comfortable with yourself, get comfortable with change. Brace yourself, there are going to be people and things constantly trying to throw you off track and it will become difficult to remain focused. I'm pretty sure a lot of us have heard that "people want you to do good, just not better than them." Understand that you don't even necessarily have to be doing better; all it takes is for someone to think you are. For example, the personality that I have shines really bright, so I have people around me that assume that because of the way that I carry myself that I'm "well off" or have "a silver spoon" in my mouth, but as you read each page, and get to know me more, you understand that I'm rich in many ways, but financially is not one of them. I literally work hard to earn every achievement. Nothing ever was or will be handed to me. That's not how it works, and I know that. I don't pretend to be better than anyone else and still find myself being the target in most situations. When you are happy, when you are positive, when you strive for greatness, when you have the universe (God) on your side, you will always be the target. I'm made out to be all of the above and then some, simply because I made the decision to pursue my dreams. Be alert realize that not everyone around you has good intentions for you. Pay close attention to what people say to you, around you, and about you. Some people know the power of their words, and will still wish things upon you out of hatred. It is so very important to keep your vibrations high at all times to defend against negative energy being released against you. Writing this for you all makes me feel so light, because I know out of every ten people that read it, I'll be changing the lives of at least nine. I realistically can't say ten, because there is always one rotten apple. At least one of those ten people are similar to the people previously described, wanting nothing but bad things for me, and the cold truth is not everyone will be chosen. Being a vessel is not all it's cracked up to be. People gravitate towards me both to be helped, and to feed off of my energy for their own selfish reasons. My job is to enlighten others and guide them along their journey to success and victory. You can and you will overcome. All you have to do is apply your entire mind, all of your heart and spirit, while in the same sense protecting them all.

Every Rose has its Thorns!

I once thought that I wouldn't be who I am today, because there are so many characteristics of mine that one wouldn't classify as "good". It wasn't until I began learning how to balance both my light and dark qualities, and accepting that both of which constructed my character that I became comfortable with the entire woman that I am. I'm still learning how not to be so hard on myself, I am human and I make mistakes just like the next person. The perfect example would be this book. I have been told that I am a free writer. So I am sure there are more than a few errors, but that will not stop me from doing what I have set out to do. The end result will be me assisting those who need assistance. Pursuing something I have always wanted to. For a long time I doubted my worth, believing that the things I want would never be, because I didn't deserve them. It's not in any way true. The things we've experienced in life don't determine our worth, who we are does. A kind soul is what I am, genuine love is what I give, and I deserve nothing short of the best the universe has to offer. I have done so many things in my past that I am not proud of, however I was oh so lost during those times. I suppressed so many things, that I sometimes forget that they actually took place. Not loving myself caused me to seek love in others. That alone caused me so much confusion and strife in my life. Emptiness was an everyday feeling, not knowing how to achieve what I was in need of. At the time I had no idea that what I was looking for was within. Despite my renewed way of thinking, I still don't have all of the answers. I understand that I can't have full control over my life, and things that happen, but I can control my reactions. Trying to convince myself to not think as much is mission impossible. My mind is always moving, in fact it sometimes moves faster than my mouth, or in this case my hands. One of the biggest things to me has always been to assist others when and where I can, however, nobody really ever does that for me. I know what it's like to feel alone, I want to be of assistance to everyone who feels that way. Growing up and always feeling like I wasn't good enough, I believed that the treatment I was receiving was what I was supposed to receive. That was it. The not so great end of the stick is what I was worth. I wanted nothing more than to escape it, and I would day dream about how I was going to do it. To have the people you love to be the ones to hurt you and cause you pain teaches you that it's acceptable to receive less. This way of thinking spread through my relationships and friendships overall. I was abused in many different forms. So much mental damage was done that I had absolutely no choice but to turn within and figure out what the problem was. In this mists of doing so, I have discovered so much pain that was buried beneath the surface. I have been let down and disappointed. I have been kicked while at my absolute lowest points. I have been made to feel as if I am not enough. So much so, that I allowed the feeling to take over my mind and started to believe that, and accept things that I shouldn't have. I was attracting that into my life by believing that was for me. I have been trying to avoid having to face those things, but the only way I'll ever be able to progress in life is by doing so. First things first, I have to let go of the negative things that have been said about and to me as they are not the blueprint of who I am.

One of my favorite things about myself is the way I love beyond conditions. So many people have hurt me, time and time again. The unfortunate thing about that is that it's the people that are the closest to me. I realized a very long time ago that I am in more ways than one misunderstood. It honestly seems to be a never ending cycle that I just want to be over. I know for a fact that I deserve more than this, I am beyond drained at this point. I continuously give my all, even when I have little to nothing to give. There are very few times where anything is given in return. Earlier in life, I was conditioned to believe that how I felt was nothing compared to whatever someone else may have felt. Not changing the way your mind works, the thoughts you have will become repetitive. Everything will be, It may even take a while before you notice it, and that's okay, it happened to me. Every day it's a struggle to remain positive, to maintain that lifestyle while everything around you seems to be going the opposite. I have slipped into darkness more than a few times before I not only paid attention, but listened to my intuition. There will always be something inside of you, speaking to you, guiding you. We all hear it; some of us just choose not to pay attention. I have allowed myself to get caught up in my feelings plenty of times, and as we know that didn't work out too well. I have literally become a prisoner to my pain. This is not where it ends though, I love myself too much. Way too many people believe that perfect exists, everything has flaws. The solution is seeing the beauty in everything. In all fairness, we all know that is easier said than done. It's a constant battle that won't change. Every day will be challenging, and if it isn't you're doing something wrong!

What's wrong with This Picture?

Dealing with ascension is not at all an easy thing to do, I often refer to it as inner purging. That is the best way to describe it, because all of these things, feelings, people etc. from the past come up to the surface one after the other or all at once and you have no choice but to face it. Correction, we all have a choice, however I chose to face all of these things head on. I got tired of repeating the same old things constantly, pure insanity. Even when I was under the impression that I was doing things differently, God stepped in and said "Nope, that's actually the same thing in a different way. Try something else." For years, I thought that I was able to run away from the problems and that running would help me defeat it. That did absolutely nothing but allow me to live in denial. I thought that not thinking of the things that I've done in my past, not associating myself with certain people anymore or not even talking about certain things would wipe the slate clean, but in all honesty the slate just got smudged. Bringing you all along this journey with me means that I am literally living these things out as you read. While writing, I have noticed many things repeating themselves, me repeating myself. There is a deeper significance to all of what you have read up to this point. The relation is to what I am speaking of right now. Regardless of how "right" you think you have it or how much of a "difference" you think your current approach is making, if you keep being negligent to what you have to handle internally, you will never, ever move on. The ultimate goal is steady progression, but if you notice things continuously happening the same as before, there is a lot of soul work that needs to be done on yourself. Don't fight it. In advance, please understand that this will, without a doubt be extremely painful and may even be confrontational. What I have discovered is that it won't be as easy to get everyone else on board and involved with your healing process as you may like it to be. There will be many different layers to this, it is not nor should you expect it to be an overnight process. Patience is very essential at this time. This coming from a woman who at one point in time had none at all. I wanted it to happen overnight, I wanted to go to bed and wake up the next morning completely healed and ready to go, but it just doesn't work that way. In fact, this process is teaching me to be patient. I am learning the beauty of diligence, and taking your time. Some people around you will have opinions on how you should go about handling situations, or what moves you should take next but at the end of the day, the only person who knows what will be more beneficial for you, is you. Don't be afraid to trust your intuition and the voice that you hear internally. Every day when faced with different obstacles, you will hear voices in your mind on which paths to choose, listen to them. Keep in mind that there are also intuitive suggestions that will come to you from a not so good or solid place, those are the ones to avoid. In life, we all have the opportunity and leisure of choosing. This is not an exclusion. You will have to trust your intuition as to what you should do. Easier said than done, just as most things in life are. The key here is to evaluate everything that you were at one point doing that got you to where you are now which is in most cases right back where you started, or stuck on one level. Ask yourself, what is it that I am doing that is not working? What can I do differently? Compare and contrast the choices you have made in the past and the choices you can make at this point and moving forward. There is no room for doubt when dealing with self-evolution. The biggest and most important key to success during this time is learning to trust yourself. Utilize the things you have gone through or experienced thus far to assist you along the way. Not to mention the ascended masters who are there just waiting for you to ask them for guidance. Let them help you!

The conflict with this can be when you feel that you strongly desire something or wish for something to happen or even for someone to be part of your life. You feel as if you have all of the answers, and know what's best for you, and then once again the most high has different plans. His agenda aligns with your purpose and life mission, whereas your plans steer you away from that. It's all essential and mandatory along this journey. In order to fulfill what you are here to, you must go through the motions. Including but not limited to failed friendships and relationships. No matter how much you may love someone, some people are literally apart of your life for the season they are to assist you with getting to the next chapter of your life. Not everyone you cross paths with is meant to stay around for the duration of your lifetime. It's okay to let go. Allow this to resonate in your mind. One you begin to let go of fears, habits, people, places and things that no longer serve a purpose to your life, you will feel and be so much lighter. The best thing you could ever do for yourself is love you better than anyone else ever could. No one will ever show you that love in return until you learn it is not something to be seeked in others, but something to find, something that already exists within each and every one of us. Every day I see more and more of the beauty around me, because

I have de-programmed myself. When we are kids, we are taught (as previously mentioned) to be a certain way, to overall think, feel, even believe certain ways and things. Since birth, we have been stripped of our individuality. Everyone started blending and melting together over time. It is okay to step outside of your comfort zone, and this time around, I am jumping out of it. Disregarding all past pain and any and all fears are being conquered. In order to progress and move forward, I must let go! Strip myself of what I have been taught to do and take back what rightfully belongs to me, ME.

Every now and again things and people from my past attempt to make a return, and unlike before, I don't allow it. No matter how much at one point I may have been attached. I am completely detaching myself from everything and everyone, and getting more so acquainted with myself than I have ever been. To be completely honest I have never felt better. For a while I thought that it was important to be there for others, and be what everyone else needed me to be, doing whatever it may have been that someone else needed me to do. However, these days, I am learning to put myself and my needs and desires first. What I have grown to realize, is that no matter how much I may want to give to the next person, if I am not at my best, I cannot help anyone else.

Rearranging old ways and habits so that the same ole' mistakes stop repeating themselves. I have noticed the pattern, spotted the problem, and now I am rectifying the situation by making the necessary changes. I am so grateful to have a few vibrant and radiant souls around me that will be as honest with me as possible, but there is no better honesty than from one's self. I am letting myself know what work needs to be done within, and I am making those things happen. You and only you will be able to do that. So ask yourself "What's wrong with this picture?" and get to editing. Remember, you are the artist, you make the final decisions, you control your happiness.

Say What You Feel and Feel What You Say

When I was younger I often felt like I had to "keep quiet" because no one would understand me. A lot of the time the thoughts and feelings I expressed were either overlooked or down played to be made out as not important or sufficient. This caused me to believe that was true, and it carried on into my relationships with people and made me much more of a people pleaser than I needed to be. I would hold on to toxic friendships, and relationships a lot longer than need be. Everyone would always be able to come to me and have me understand or be there for them, this continued for years, for as long as I can remember. That is until recently, when I decided that my mental, emotional and spiritual health was beneficial. Interesting fact of it all is it happened because I recognized my love for being there for others. I know that if I am not in a good space, I cannot be at my best for others. I have been advising people for years to put their selves first and get their selves in order, yet I put off loving me to focus on loving and assisting others. Ultimately, that would leave me without, feeling drained, used and abused. I recognized what needed to be done in order to be of full service to and for others, so that's what I have been doing. This chapter is about taking your own advice. It's one thing to constantly have all of the answers and always be there for others, but what good is that if you are not living proof? I prefer to be and do what I tell others to be and do.

Along these last few months, I have lost a lot of people and surprisingly, I took it with a grain of salt and let it be what it is. Reason being, anyone who is not willing to be understanding towards you working on becoming a better you does not need to be around you to begin with. Those people who have fallen off the grid in my life have been replaced by people with really amazing souls who I feel were brought to me through the most high. They have been extremely helpful and supportive during my journey. I don't get anything but positive energy and feedback from these individuals, with the exclusion of. For a very long time, I knew what I should be doing with my life was helping others in an unconditionally loving way, but I was lacking the unconditional love for myself. I had to get myself together, which I am still in the process of doing in order to be able to contribute to someone else's soul. I cannot heal broken hearts with broken hands.

The most difficult struggle during this time in my life is balancing the light and dark within myself. I wouldn't dare sit here and pretend to be something or someone I am not, that's not even my style. I would much rather be an open book so that the people I am supposed to help will get the help they deserve. I have lied, cheated, stolen things, I have done very, very bad things in my life thus far, but none of that alters the type of heart that I have. What so many people tend to forget is that the wrong or bad that you either do now or have done at one point or another does not make you a bad person. Good people do bad things, only difference is who gets caught out there and who doesn't. I seeked validation from others, under the impression that it would make me feel better about myself, the cache 22 there, is that when they don't like you or no longer favor you, their opinions and feelings towards you can tear you down.

When I look back on everything that has transpired, I sit in awe at some of the things that I did. I realize how very lost I was, and am often shocked that I didn't realize it sooner. Why is that? Why did I not realize that I was living a life of destruction no matter what people around me would say? It's because I was blinded and smothered in my pain. Allowing the things that I've been through, or the people who caused me grief to have the upper hand over me and my life. I was so busy trying to get away from it, aiming to suppress it, that I had not realized that I was just burying myself in it. It wasn't until I decided to remove my hands from over my eyes to face the harsh reality that I created for myself that I began to heal. I have spent many nights in sorrow, trying to cry, but not being able to. Yes, it had gotten that bad. I was not able to cry, I had literally trained myself to just deal with it. Therefore, I was unable to fully heal, and that's all I wanted. No matter how sad I was, no matter how much it hurt, I could not cry.

If you have never experienced that feeling, let's just say it is by far the worst. You don't know what to do or how you will ever feel better again. I dug deep into my soul to focus on the things that have caused this, I wanted to stare at them face to face and confront my demons, fears, and hurt head on so that's what I did. I planned on writing letters to whomever need be and tossing them somewhere, instead I have been able to speak with some of them and have very much so needed conversations, including but not limited to myself. I would look myself in the mirror and speak to and from within. One very much so needed convoy that has come to pass is that with my mother. For the first time ever, she listened. She did not interrupt, or cut me off to tell me how "crazy I am", she did not belittle my feelings or thoughts, she simply listened. And not only did she listen, she understood. I cannot begin to explain how amazing that felt, or what that has done for me. My mom is the person I always wanted to impress, but always seemed to fall short of doing so. To come to grips with not being perfect, not always satisfying others, including her, and genuinely placing my happiness first is the best thing I have ever felt besides being a mother of course.

As some of you may know, there is nothing in this world that compares to being someone's mother. I can honestly say that working on myself, recapturing my innocence and vulnerability has opened my heart in so many ways, including aiding me with motherhood. Children go off of energy and how people's energy feels to them, my son has been gravitating towards me a lot more these days. Kisses and hugs for days, I even get woken up to them. Part of why I have decided to get me together, is for the sake of my son. He did not ask to be here, although I do feel it was a pre-arranged agreement (for those of you who understand what I mean); therefore, it is my job to instill great qualities in him. Meaning, mommy has to be an amazing example. When he comes to me to tell me what he wants to do, what he aspires to do, he will know that he can, because he will see that mommy did.

Intuition is so strong, but somehow we often choose to ignore it. Don't. Whenever you feel something, go with it. If you feel it in your gut that you shouldn't be doing something or shouldn't entertain someone, listen. There has been entirely too many times I was faced with choosing something and decided for whatever reason to go against my instinct. Whenever I chose not to listen, the outcome was awful. Remember how I discussed earlier the importance of learning the lesson from the experience so that you can apply it towards future endeavors? This is one of the many things that applies to.

As I mature spiritually, I recognize all of what helped mold me into the queen I am now. However I do understand that a lot of those things could have been avoided and caused a lot of setbacks to my growth. It wasn't until I realized it and started moving differently that things started improving. Once I accepted full ownership of my bullshit, it became so much easier to progress. Accepting responsibility of your actions will be beneficial in the long run as it is also helpful during the present.

Love, Lust and Other Distractions

It is important to know your worth. No one else is going to believe in you the way that you do, and that's more than okay. Stand firmly for what you believe in because anything is possible. I had to learn my worth, and fall in love with myself unconditionally. Fear and the feeling of loneliness got me to a point of utter sadness. Although I am confident, optimistic, and meticulous, I have experienced my fair share of doubts and what I call "low points" just like anyone else. Somewhat believing that what I needed was in someone else, I was so confused and lost. I allowed myself to be mistreated by people I loved that I trusted at one point or another because, I was so busy trying to please everyone else that I forgot about my happiness. What really matters to me? Somewhere along the way I become complacent and willing to have and be the average. Despite me knowing I deserved to be treated better. I made the mistake of allowing fear to prevent me from doing what I've always wanted to do. Ultimately, I just wanted to be happy. The ways I went about achieving that though were highly incorrect.

I was searching for love in other people when I didn't have the unconditional love for myself. With that comes me having mistaken lust and the bare minimum for love and everything it really is. I always knew that what I wanted existed, I just didn't know it was within all along. They made it seem as if what I was asking was too much, when I on the other hand, did it with ease. Then one day, just like that it hit me. Refusing to put others first, satisfying everyone else while crumbling away internally just wasn't going to work. It wasn't enough. It never was, and never will be enough. When it came to relationships, there are only three guys that I have ever truly cared for. All three of those guys showed me that although I displayed the love I wanted to receive in return, I wasn't displaying it towards and for myself. Why would one allow this to happen three times? Having a humongous heart and giving the wrong people entirely too many chances. Love is unconditional, but in order to properly give that to others, you have to begin within yourself. Now that I am aware of what I was doing wrong, I have ceased it in order to correct it.

Apparently, I have thick skin! People have called me out of my name, in attempts to belittle me. I have never allowed it to deteriorate my souls inner walls, but there has been a few days in the past where I would be upset, frustrated, angered, or sad just by letting things I knew weren't true temporarily get the upper hand. It is so important to stand firm, and be strong all the while keeping your head high. This is what I want you to get out of this. You don't need anyone else to make you whole, as you are that all by yourself. Anything that someone else could offer or bring to your table are additional, as it should be for them with what you offer and bring to their table. Both individuals involved should be this way with their selves because in order to attract it, you have to be it. You cannot love someone completely if you don't even know how to love yourself completely.

During my teenage years I was so lost and so confused. Elementary school on to high school I was made fun of for being different. The other girls would taunt and tease me saying things like "she swears she's so cute.", or "she thinks she's better than everyone else." I developed at an early age, so my body was always a little more mature than I was. The guys noticed, and were all over me like flies on a pile of shit. Despite how uninterested I was, that changed nothing. Hormonal little boys and a girl who looks the way I did was not a good combination. In fact, because of the panting that would go on even more girls didn't like me. It created so much hatred towards me, as to where I wouldn't even have to do or say anything, someone wanted to attack me because "they didn't like me." To this day I don't understand what I did that caused others to want to harm me, besides being myself. There were rumors and terrible lies spread and for years this continued. I had a very tough period of secretly battling low self-esteem.

I started to confide in this one person. Someone I could talk to about how I felt, and this person would make me laugh and feel good about myself. They also gave me the feeling of being safe whenever they were around. I felt protected. I never felt pressured to be or do more than I wanted to, which being a teenager with raging hormones of my own made me want to do more. Want to feel more. I was young and with this person for a couple of years without even feeling pushed into having sex. This was big to me, because everyone around us was doing it. That and me being foolish enough to think it was a fairy tale decided to give my innocence to this person. I allowed myself to be deflowered because I thought I was in love. I went against my own beliefs, and let go of the way I always thought it would happen for me. I felt like the odd man out and was tired of feeling like that. I gave myself to this person only to discover they were nothing close to my happy ending. We were together for four years. Then one day, I was walking home from his house, and I got to thinking. I was over it, I wasn't about to waste anymore of my time trying to hold on to someone because of the mistake I made. I had to put my big girl drawls on, and understand that my poor decision of a choice was not the determining factor of how the rest of my life will go. I am so much more than that and I deserve more than a situation that isn't fair to either party. We were both young and had so much living to do. I stopped answering text messages and phone calls and just completely distanced myself. It was necessary in order to disconnect.

Anyone in between him and the next person I actually had feelings for were people I hung out with a few times here and there. Maybe there was some kind of attraction, but it wasn't consisting of anything more than that. We may have even had a good time or two, but that's all it was. So if you're reading this and realize you don't fit the description of either person mentioned, or anyone in this story, there are no hard feelings. I just have to be honest with myself. With that will come truth being revealed, and in a nutshell it is what it is. I have only let my walls come down for these people.

The next guy came after high school, the fall after to be exact. He came into my life during a really low point, where I felt stuck in between who I use to be, and who I was at that time. Far from your average drug dealer, he was romantic, sweet, charming, funny and intelligent. He was in college, trying to make more of himself, but he was faced with challenges of his own. At that time in both of our lives, things were difficult at home. Neither one of us was getting along too well with our parents. Me because, I have always been independent, wanting to try and do things my way. Him because, his family felt he wasn't contributing enough despite him giving as much as he possibly could. We were both so stressed from our living situations that we gravitated towards each other. We were each other's peace. Where ever you saw me, you saw him and vice versa. I loved him so much, my friends and family loved him as well. We would smoke refer and talk about life, political science, and things going on in our community. Watch funny movies, take long walks or long spontaneous car rides, he's actually who taught me how to drive. I and his family however, did not get along. His mother and father would address me as "that girl", and his sister felt as if he should've been in a relationship with someone else. Despite that, his grandmother loved me, and to this day asks about me, and his nieces love me too! We made plans on leaving all of the chaos behind and starting anew somewhere in the south, as we both eventually wanted to go down there. We had the game plan all figured out. His family planted into his brain that he was foolish to only be taking one young woman seriously. The ways he would hurt me, would be by emotionally and mentally cheating on me with other girls. There was inappropriate conversation going on, and when I would catch wind of it, we would get into it. Our fights would be huge, but because I was blinded by emotions, I stayed in the relationship. Around this time, things had started going downhill at home for me in a rapid manner. It got so bad, that I decided to go stay in North Carolina with my uncle. Despite me moving away, we chose to stay together. The plan was for him to come down and see me as often as he could. Often enough to keep the relationship going. The first time he came down to see me, was unfortunately the last. While he was down there, everything was great. I still had to work, so when I would get off, he would be outside of my job waiting for me. We would walk back down to the apartment, and just have an amazing time enjoying each other's company. One day while eating breakfast, his phone rang. Instead of him answering it or replying to the messages, he looked at it and then hurried to place it face down. That let me know something was up. When I asked to see it, he was for the first time ever hesitant. No matter how many times I asked. He appeared nervous. I grabbed the phone, that's when I saw the messages. It became very clear what had happened. I asked him if he had sex with this other young woman, he insisted on telling me no repetitively. I then asked him to call this girl on the phone and have her verify (let's pause). This is something I would never in a million years do now, because I have found myself completely. I know what I deserve and a young man who is not willing to give me that is not worth the trouble. (Play)... He didn't want to, so I did. I called her, she answered, and everything paused for a moment. The phone was on speaker, I told him to ask her how it was. Reason being someone who's never been sexually active with you will be so confused. Her response was "what do you mean?" He then said "the sex", her response took the cake. "I can't talk about that right now, because I'm around family." After that, I was mentally uninvolved in the situation.

He was the first man to break down all of my walls. I was completely open with him about everything. My fears, desires, and everything in between. It's not unrealistic for people to fall in love and start a life at the age we were then. At only 18, being so open with him, having similar standards in which we lived and were raised by. I don't doubt that he loved me, he was just young and not mentally prepared to face temptation. Especially with his girl being hours and states away. Once I found out what I needed to know, I instantly got mad. I'm not going to sit here and lie to any of you. I messed him up. It's like something came over me, all I saw was red, and I attacked. I started to kick him and all of his belongings out of the apartment. I actually did. Then felt bad, because although he cheated on me and broke my trust, he was in North Carolina with me being the only person he knew in Chapel Hill. I welcomed him back in. He wanted to talk, so we did. I was not mentally involved with him anymore, because all I could think of was what he did, but my heart was still very much so involved with him.

When I came back to New Jersey, it was sudden. The plan was to come visit friends for a weekend, but things happened that caused me to stay here while all of my things were left behind. All of which you know at this point. It didn't take long for me to come to the realization that I couldn't get over what he did to me. I needed to be by myself for a while. The pain displayed by him could've made any sane woman think twice about the decision. Nonetheless, it was necessary.

I started to finally get myself together. My parents and I talked everything out, and I was back with them. The difference this time was I gained a little more maturity, knew how it felt to make nothing out of something for myself, and was determined to get my life back on track. I held tight to my list of goals (short, mid, and long term). That living situation lasted for all of 6 months before I decided to try living on my own. I wanted the experience, but I didn't have the resources to obtain it lavishly. There was an ad in the local supermarket for available bedrooms in a home in a nearby city. I decided to go check it out. Although it wasn't and may not be much to some people, I was 20 gaining life experiences that most don't until they're in their late 20's. I had the job, I had the car, and I had somewhere to lay my head at night that I was responsible for paying for. I was uncomfortable at first, but got used to it after a while. After all I did move to a completely different state, miles and hours away from all of my friends, family and all that I knew and made things happen. I could do it here too. The only problem was, it wasn't going to happen with $7.25 an hour. Something had to give. I found a better job, making a little more, and it still wasn't enough. Determined to make it work, I held on until I couldn't anymore. Eventually I had to take a few steps back, and move along. A close friend of mine and I tried rooming together for a minimum of 3 weeks before we realized that just wasn't it. I went back home, yet again. I can't possibly explain how it felt this time around. Enough was enough. I had to press restart and try it again. I found an even better job, something more suitable for me and my skills. While working there, I came in contact with the last love.

What started out simply as a work out buddy, someone to walk around the track with became a whole lot of something else. After the first day linking up and talking for hours, we began seeing more of each other. When I say more, I mean on a daily basis. I would come over after work and we would play video games, work out, and have the most random conversations. There was a level of understanding there that I had never experienced before, and before I know it, this person became my shoulder to weep on and I became his. I enjoyed the time we spent together. The understanding we had caused the illusion of it being us against the world. I remember him telling me about how he was on hard times at the moment, but I chose to see the good within the same way I prefer for others to see it when it comes to me. Everyone has fallen on hard times, I didn't want to believe the worst about someone, knowing everything I went through myself. What I didn't know was that it was as bad as it was, that is until someone very dear to him felt the need to let me know. Several people actually. Now where I can honestly say I messed up, is not following my gut. Once I found out that he fabricated the situation, it made me feel like he couldn't possibly be honest about anything else. Despite the fact though, I threw caution to the wind and decided to proceed with caution. Apparently I wasn't cautious enough, because I got led down a very, very dark and twisted path. I was so blinded by the fact that I genuinely cared for him, that I once again put myself on the back burner and got left with nothing. The same person being referred to is the father of my son, for that reason I will keep plenty of things disclosed during this time. At the end of the day, he is now family and my loyalty is to my family. We have an understanding to this day in regards to our roles in our child's life, and that is where we keep it.

Knowing the things that I do now, I understand that just because a person is sincere with others doesn't mean that they will be sincere with you in return. When it comes to relationships or "situationships" as we call them these days, understand that people will pretend to be all that you want to appeal to you. Eventually the true characteristics will surface, and you will have the opportunity to see exactly what and who you are dealing with. This is the reason why you should build friendships with people prior to even thinking of beginning something deeper with them. The ugly truth is not everyone is "deep", so how can they have something as such? Mission impossible. Speaking from experience, if the priorities are not in line as they should be, dating should be the last thing on your mind. Working on pursuing my dreams, my only focus has been completing tasks that will make those dreams my reality. There has always been several people interested, this time around though, I am not thinking of having any relationships. They are there, and my way of thinking is simple. If they are meant for me, they will meet me at the finish line.

I am still residing in this body, I am human and I do crave flesh near mine just as anyone does. I have had my share of lustful flings as well, something I am not embarrassed or ashamed of. I don't believe in sexist ways of thinking. Just as a man feels he can do these things, women can, and we do. I will be one of the first people to discuss these things freely, because I do not see anything wrong with living as long as it does not throw you off of your game, which when I was younger, I was not mentally prepared to handle. Therefore, sometimes those things would become distracting to me. Whenever I was stressed beyond capacity, I would release. That side of me that I now have control over would come out to play. I refuse to let anyone distract me or throw me off. What that means, is that whenever I have those feelings I dive into my work. I utilize my energies carefully now understanding the many layers of the exchange of energy. All of me is currently on reserve for the King to this Queen, until then its continuous progression. That is my only focus!

Prioritize, Progress, Accept and Release!

A Girl is confused in a world where everything is already written. My advice to her would be to proceed with looking forward. A lot easier said than done, I know, but that is where one finds success. Utilize the lessons that have been taught, let them be the answer whenever you're confused. Remember to ask for guidance as the ascended masters are always near and willing to assist. Yet another lesson I had to learn recently. Be not afraid of the unknown; let it be as beautiful as it is. I see the beauty in everything, I've always allowed myself to feel, but I have never felt this deep. These days, I am allowing myself to be vulnerable and accepting the feelings and experiences along the journey thereafter. Doing so has me more in tune with my feminine energy than ever. Definitely a wonderful feeling to be honest, being comfortable with being a nurturer, being a mother, being a healer, being focused. It is during the darkest times that you will have absolutely no choice but to find the light within. Once my light started shining, there was nothing I could do, nothing that could happen, that could turn it down. As we grow older, we gain more responsibilities; we get more on our plate that we need to take care of. Along the way the situations we have to deal with throw us off track. One of the most tedious tasks is remaining focused when you have everything under the sun being utilized as a pawn to distract you from what really matters. This is a general statement that I feel more so pertains to "young adults" trying to organize their lives. Once again balance is essential, let go of or remove toxic situations and people from your life, and narrow in on what has priority over others.

Some people have always referred to me as a "grandma" and until now, I never understood why. I like to go out, have a good time and enjoy myself just like the next person. I am nowhere near a stranger to messing up or stumbling every now and again. What helps me remain focused is centering in on or figuring out what my goals are, and then I place them in order of importance. One by one, I go down the list checking things off as I go along. There has been times where achieving one accomplishment would take longer than others, but nevertheless, it got done!

Once those things are completed, I create an entirely new list of goals. It's a never ending cycle, it's infinite. There is always something to learn, meaning there will always be a new lesson to apply, and meaning there will always be an obstacle to overcome and a goal to achieve. Discipline is mandatory in all of this, without it you are more than likely to remain stagnant. When you are completely uncomfortable, you're doing it right. I never want to be comfortable, that's how people get lazy. I'm far too driven to ever allow that. Most of the time, it is us who restricts ourselves from achieving greatness. We allow the doubt to overpower the possibilities of success. Once you learn to release and let go of everything that no longer serves a purpose, you will find bliss. Create your magical space in your head. What would your bliss consist of? Live it, and so be it.

Step into Your Personal Power

Don't allow the pressure to push you into something other than what you want. Be real with yourself and the things you desire! Once you gravitate, meditate, manifest, believe, achieve- repeat! Your heart, let it speak for you without restrictions and made up limitations. Express freely, be courageous as you assist those that may need to know the things that you know. Allow it to overflow and become contagious. Unleash your mind as it roams freely; appreciate all of the beauty you recognize within and around you. Breathe it in, the crisp air travel down your air ways, suddenly you're aware and what had been taken away and twice removed, three times over is visible, you see reality. They took it away and hid it underneath the programs, but you refuse to get with the program, so you find the remote and you change the channel. Valuable time wasted? No, you experienced life journeys that gave great lessons in exchange of your hurt feelings. All of which you can store, and apply when necessary. Don't fight it, it's needed. Be love and light for those that need it. Embrace everything that got you to where you are. When the memory of some of those things makes you frown, come back to the here and now and count your blessings. All that you have is all that you need. Appreciate what you already have, and you will receive more. Whatever you want can be yours, but you have to go after it as if your livelihood depended on it. Open up your heart to love those that need to be loved.

After so long of repeating a cycle, you should have learned from the mistakes along the way. Instead of looking for this love that I know exists, that I deserve, I'm going to focus all of my energy on myself and becoming greater! I have an amazing gift, I love beyond limitation. The pain I've experienced throughout the years has never altered that in anyway. I strongly agree with the saying "whatever you put out, you will receive." So anyone that has done wrong by me, whether it's family, friends or someone who was once of significance – that's on them. It will all come back full circle.

Karma – N: The sum of a person's actions in this and previous states of existence, viewed as deciding their fate in future existences.

I have always and will always say "be careful how you treat people". I would hate to come off as cocky in any way, but any and every one from my past has always tried to come back. Maybe because genuine is hard to find nowadays. People are way too focused on trying to appeal to others as opposed to getting familiar with all that they are, what makes them happy, and being their best possible selves. I am not in any way judging as it has taken me this long to apply the knowledge. I had to teach myself that unfortunately no matter how much you want to believe in people or give them a chance, not everyone deserves that opportunity. Not everyone deserves to get to know you on that level of intimacy. You have to call it what it is, getting to know me is an opportunity of a lifetime.

You have to acknowledge and thoroughly understand that there is only one you! Nobody can be you or even come close. Recognize all of the amazing things about yourself and continuously strive to make them even better than they already are. Understand that everyone can start anew. For every day that you open your eyes, is a chance to try again. My past is not in any way squeaky clean, but that's more than okay. All of who, what, and how I use to be constructed the woman that I am, and who I am now is preparing me for the Queen I am transitioning into. I wear my wounds proudly. They let it be known without me even having to say so, that no matter what is thrown at me regardless of obstacles I am faced with, I will survive and I will continuously get better and stronger. The pain is beneficial to your growth and evolution. You have to be willing to put in the work to get where you would like to go, endure the struggle. It doesn't matter if you experience being homeless, heart break after heart break, if you and your family aren't getting along. It doesn't matter if everything in the world just seems to be pulling and weighing down on you all at one time, you have to continuously run after what you want. If that means running with bricks tied around your ankles so be it, you keep running.

www.ingramcontent.com/pod-product-compliance
Lightning Source LLC
Chambersburg PA
CBHW020024050426
42450CB00005B/639